The

KYTE

Book of

Modern and

PostModern

Quotations

Mel Reichler
&
Jim Egan

THE ORIGINS OF THIS BOOK

Jim Egan and I tried to publish the books we wrote. We harassed books publishers, publishers of stories, publishers of tracts, publishers of scraps and flotsam — to no avail. After this continued and long lasting self-flagellation we decided what we needed was a kite book a book which would fly strong and high and carry all of the books we had written, individually and collectively, as its tail, to fame and fortune. Unfortunately none of the books we had written could be coaxed to do this onerous work. The absence of a kite book weighed on us heavily.

The idea finally came to us that if we needed a kite book we could make a kite book, a book whose sole purpose was to fly straight up, as high as it could fly, and carry its brothers and sisters with it. It was one of those desperate, creative ideas that imposes itself without reason. So this kite book was invented, not out of whole cloth but out of some cloth, a mashup, "a history of the Jews before there were Jews," as Reb Dunzel would say, a desperate invention in a time that calls for desperate inventions.

If the internet had existed when we were younger, when we were producing our opuses perhaps we would not have been in this predicament. As it is desperate times, the times of tin men, cellphoned men and aids, desperate measures are called for. Hence, the KYTE book. It represents us at our most creative (not that that counts for much.) It contains little mind knittings that deserve to be preserved and better known than they are; not all of them but some.

Mel Reichler Jim Egan

Here is the TAIL of the KYTE (a list of the books we have written.)

By Mel Reichler & Jim Egan
Corkscrews (part of this book is in the KYTE book)
The Man with the Ladder Stories, Vol 1 & Vol2

By Jim Egan
Secrets we have Kept from Ourselves

By Mel Reichler
The Chistmas Stories
Vermeers
Book of Common Wisdom Vol 1 & Vol2 (included in the KYTE book)
Virtual Soho
The Granddaughter Books (including Maya's First Books & Ashley in the Computer.)
The Collected Stories
The Complete Musicals
Songs, Uncommon Prayers, Poems

By Mel Reichler and Tom Surprenant
Information

In the end most of us are reduced to imitating ourselves.

Darkness also travels at the speed of light.

Rub the thorn, remember the knife.

Those who want to, shouldn't. Those who will, can't. Those who should, may not. Those who can, won't. We are always having to choose between getting things done not quite well enough and getting them done at all.

Armies never surrender at night.

It is important to distinguish what you need from what you want. It is even more important to distinguish what you want from what you want to want. But what is most important of all, is to distinguish what you want badly from what you want badly, but not badly enough.

The Quotations of RD

Darkness also travels at the speed of light.

Every truth finds its way blocked by a reasonable desire.

Buffalos don't come with brakes.

We never think about stopping a large object when it is standing still.

Things that are easy to lose are hard to find.

The disaster of some people's lives is that they fall in love with their first mistake instead of their second.

Waking up is the best proof you've been asleep.

Death has a slogan: return the empties.

What God really wanted to forbid he made physically impossible to do.

When friends separate God puts away the locusts and chastises only with butterflies.

Safe is never virtuous.

People who demand the impossible may be satisfied with the improbable, and he who asks for what he can not have must settle for what he is not likely to get.

Sex is a pleasure; good sex is pleasure; great sex is what pleasure is about.

A sacred cow makes a bad pet.

The heart of any spoken truth is a feeling that cannot be put into words.

Truth is just the best available metaphor at any given time.

If you learn to read between the lines you can read anything, in almost any language.

Reality stands behind its illusions.

There are days that never appear anywhere but on calendars and then only after the fact, and there are other days that appear and reappear on privy doors and subway posters and the backs of animals and children's drawings and in beer advertisements on T.V., so that they feel like they have been lived in again and again like an old house that has been occupied for centuries.

Death does not keep records, at least not good records. Of course it does not have to.

Pleasure which cannot be enjoyed may have to be endured.

Believing should be a matter of choice, disbelieving a matter of necessity.

Events and the memory of events change at different rates. The memory of an event changes at the same rate as the consequences of an event. Events change a little more quickly than the anticipation of the consequences.

Most things have a short end and an long end.

Sometimes there is no shortest distance between two points.

Some people need a reason before they act, others need an excuse.

A reason is an excuse before its time.

A lie is a reason that appeared only after the fact.

Shrewdness is always limited by deceit.

The many should not be encouraged by the victories of the few. On the other hand the few should take no comfort in having succeeded where the many have not, for those who climb high upon the backs of others discover it is a very precarious perch.

Happiness is Boolean.

People seldom survive the bite of a butterfly. On the other hand the scars of the bite of the butterfly are beautiful.

Some people crave to be a good servant but can't find a good master.

The strength of the Japanese is not in any particular Japanese.

Everyone has a good side and a bad side. Unfortunately, some people's good side belongs to someone else.

All of us are crazy but some of us wear our straight jackets only on formal occasions.

The unbelievable occurs regularly—but no one believes it.

Intelligence sucks and wisdom spits out.

Sex is a palace with neither an exit nor an entrance, only a window.

Sex makes a better vice than a virtue.

Only in sex can two people be separated from one another by the thickness of their skins and yet be worlds apart.

Man becomes more like the machines he uses than the food he eats.

Sex makes love bearable.

We are indebted to unnamed sexual heroes.

At the heart of every illusion is a misplaced conviction that reality is a good master.

Pre-remembered sex is often better than remembered sex.

Sex is a metaphor for all other metaphors.

Good sex is the only defense against bad sex.

There is a kind of medicine pigeons practice on fleas.

Youth is filled with deprivations and injustice and pain. What makes it youth is that it is ignorant of them.

Ignore virtue and you create a vice.

You can recognize a fool even when he's fooling around.

Folly is intelligence with a thorn in its paw.

One does not become a fool at a ceremony. Even so, every ceremony creates its own fool.

To the color blind folly is gray. With acute sight we see that it is bright gray.

We remember only the original and the latest folly, but only the latest folly counts.

Sometimes being wrong is the only available relief from being uncertain.

If you can't trust your own eyes whose eyes can you trust.

No wonder we have trouble saying what we mean. We must do all our talking with second hand words.

Some people have a larger vocabulary than they have words to say it in.

Contrary to common sense there are no spaces between words. Like the real numbers the spaces between real words are filled with imaginary words. The word line is dense.

There is nothing so frustrating as a day that goes back on its promise.

Some people promise high quality frustration and provide low quality relief.

The logic of surrender is simple: throw up your hands. The logic of complete surrender is simpler: throw up.

Panic is crying for help with your feet.

Great novelists die in other people's sleep.

We always know one character from a great novel personally.

What is impossible is forbidden: anything else you can get away with is permitted.

Just because it's been said for the second time doesn't mean you heard it the first or will hear it the third.

Experience leaves too much to the imagination to be trusted.

The virtuous whore is the invention of the virtuous pimp.

A saint is a man who is willing to share his pleasure without demanding that you share his pain—but has no pleasure to share.

Creative irrationality is art's reason.

Normality is nothing more than the current standard and style of being irrational.

10 O'clock is always predictable but no one really knows what time 12 o'clock will come next.

Some jobs that really need to be done aren't for the simple reason that people make you pay to do them and then make you pay again to do them well. Other jobs that really need to be done aren't for the simpler reason that the person who sees the need is not the person who must do the work to satisfy it.

In the end most of us are reduced to imitating ourselves.

The best conversation is about things we can't talk about.

The best reasons make the worst excuses.

News is gossip we can all agree upon.

Some people's lives are based on a true story but not their true story.

People we don't know are just as perplexed as people we do.

Money is always in heat.

The only dollar bill with a pedigree is a counterfeit.

Some people's reputation leads a richer life than they do.

In the beginning and the end, lovers win.

Each of us is furious when our ideas sound better in someone else's sentences.

Every good idea is equally distant from a bad idea and a great idea.

Life has no end, it is limited only by our attention span.

It is bizarre that people will believe anything as long as you can prove it to them.

Truths come with handles; unfortunately this means that any idiot can grab hold of them.

Just because a thing is easy to do, doesn't mean it will be done well.

People tend not to notice easy things that are done well.

The great law of human nature is: if you can catch it, you can eat it.

Anatomy defeats fantasy.

No ones mind is completely civilized territory.

We are often badly served by those we serve.

We speak the way computers think; linearly, directly and completely missing the point.

Given the laws of probability an impossible event is likely to occur at any moment.

She provided grief instantly, and she guaranteed it for years to come.

The impulse to do the impossible is quite weak.

Doing the impossible is easy, it is wanting to do the impossible that is impossible.

Small pains are always available as a reminder of big pains.

N.Y.C. is a great place to visit permanently but no one wants to live there.

Corkscrews are lost point down and found point up.

The Quotations of MWL

It may be true that, in the long run, a group can survive by doing the wrong thing for the right reason as well as it can survive by doing the right thing for the wrong reason. It is questionable whether the long run includes tomorrow.

Armies never surrender at night.

The bailiff knows Murphy's law better than the judge.

Those who want to, shouldn't. Those who will, can't. Those who should, may not. Those who can, won't. We are always having to choose between getting things done not quite well enough and getting them done at all.

There are places steeped in so deep and profound an anarchy that even Murphy's law does not hold.

The best things in life may be free but the store is always out of them and they spoil when you take them out of the box, and you can't claim them as dependents on your income tax returns, whereas the worst things in life cost ferociously but are deductible, and available on easy credit, and are childlike and cling and never grow up.

Graffiti is three dimensional wisdom on a two dimensional wall.

In a pinch you can use a hammer as a screwdriver but only once per screw.

In New York, 'Alice in Wonderland' is a historical romance.

Even truth can leave you unprepared for reality and feeling that you've been deceived.

It is important to distinguish what you need from what you want. It is even more important to distinguish what you want from what you want to want. But what is most important of all, is to distinguish what you want badly from what you want badly, but not badly enough.

Big things change because people are too smart for their own good. Little things change because they are not smart enough.

If you can't come to terms with reality you have the wrong terms.

Life, like death is sleight of hand, only a little faster.

Competition is always imperfect where it counts the most.

Pleasure as well as pain, leaves scars.

Commuting is not traveling anywhere. Neither is shuffling.

Saying something, saying something in so many words, and saying something in any words at all, are quite different things.

Blessed are those who can say what they mean because not being able to say what you had in mind is a fact of mind.

Every stick has a short end and a long end. The short end of the stick is always available.

Bad spelling and tragedy don't mix.

A style of life is a poor metaphor for a way of being.

A perfect bullet can not be shot from anything less than the perfect gun. Inventing the perfect bullet is easy. Inventing the perfect gun, impossible.

For some people it is a pleasure to be caught between a rock and a hard place.

Simplicity in sex is profound.

The prick has no memory. On the other hand, the cunt never forgets.

Any doctor who refuses to believe in divine intervention and miracles foregoes 2/3rds of the tools of his trade.

The father remembers all his son's follies: The son remembers all his father's follies but one.

We can resist temptation only by convincing ourselves that we will miss the very last train home. We give into temptation when we remember that we have legs and can walk.

We remember how our foolishness feels and how other people's foolishness looks.

Foolishness is never terminal.

Sensibility seldom lies outright—but it hardly ever tells the truth either.

No given collection of words can support their own weight.

Given any collection of words, a good writer can always take one out and a bad writer put one in.

One may refuse to be frustrated only up to a point.

No event, however painful, lasts forever. It is no consolation however: the memory of pain lasts a little longer than forever.

It is possible to father a hero when what you think you are doing is having a little fun.

The mechanism we have for resisting temptation is oiled with the temptations we have given in to.

A sentence may be incoherent yet perfectly intelligible. On the other hand, it may be clear as a bell and incomprehensible.

Sometimes quitting when you're ahead is the only way of losing badly.

Great novels have at least three endings only one of which appears in the novel.

In a great novel we are likely to show up as a peripheral character.

Stealing the egg does not get you the goose.

Writers have as much control over words as stock brokers do stocks.

You can not master great literature. You can always ask it politely however.

Maturity falls on some people like a stone. Other people trip on it on the way to the bathroom.

Ask and you shall be given, don't ask and you'll get it anyway. Run away and you will trip on it, stand still and it will fall on you. The inevitable happens whether you like it or not and usually when you're looking the other way.

A country's rationality does not depend on any particular person being rational at any given time, nor does it require that everyone be rational all the time, only that some people be rational some of the time. Even with this it is remarkable how few countries are rational.

Modern electronic technology has made commonplace possible what only freak, tragic, accidents of nature accomplished before: it has made it possible to march to a different drummer,– in a different ear, in stereo, at the same time.

There is a fundamental asymmetry about the world. The only reason we do not see it is because the shift from one imbalance to another occurs to quickly to be seen.

Writing down something foolish doesn't make you foolish any more than writing down something intelligent makes you intelligent, although why this is so no one knows.

The greedy get the most of the worst of the best of any possible world or the most of the best of the worst of any possible world and they enjoy it least—because they are greedy.

When the cost of a steak is more than the price of the cow we are in trouble.

Complete indifference is as close to Godliness as one is likely to come in one's life.

A nation has absolutely collapsed when it has to import its common diseases the way it imports its television sets—and from the same place.

Most of the news that's fit to print is not fit to read.

There are games you can't win but can't lose either. These are the games without rules that are the most difficult to play.

Money is the dark phase of love. It is capable of tender mercies.

Change is collective pretend.

If you are not part of the problem you can't be part of the solution. Of course, if you are not part of the problem you probably have no interest in the solution, by which fact you become part of the problem. This is why the 70's were rapidly followed by the 90's.

A woodpecker won't peck until it smells the bark of the tree.

Reality makes things true but advertising makes them real.

No object that has been lost twice is worth looking for a third time.

It now takes all of western technology to teach a watch to tick.

Doubt lives in the shadow that every truth casts.

Life is a jig saw puzzle in which some pieces fit with every other piece and some pieces don't fit with any other piece.

Flattery is beneath contempt, usually with her legs spread and breathing hard.

At least one piece of the puzzle is always missing.

Human inefficiency on a grand scale is what makes a nation great and a people small.

A Corkscrew is the common ground between any truth and its contradiction.

Even the simplest of relationships are hopelessly complex.

If you can't be young be enthusiastic.

The Druids are here.

Genius is enthusiasm for the incomprehensible.

Love is the incomprehensibly beautiful with teeth.

Great art is always the negation of a great void.

F C Quotations

For the ant, wisdom is not walking on sidewalks even if the cracks are filled with candy and cake.

Pleasures from which there is no respite are worse than pains from which one can flee.

The improbable is merely the impossible with a license.

Wisdom is just intelligence waiting for a person to happen to.

Sometimes the end of your rope is only an inch off the ground.

To recover from an incurable illness tempts fate unnecessarily.

Every truth breaks a chain.

Every truth worth knowing can be said in no more than fifteen words. And any truth that can be said in no more than fifteen words can be said in six or less. Of course, any truth that can be said in six words or less is so obvious that it doesn't need to be spoken of at all. (It is also clear that truths that are so obvious they don't need to be spoken of, require no fewer than three volumes to write down.)

What creativity lacks in imagination it makes up.

No truth is ever spoken clearly. But then no truth is ever said twice without extensive corrections.

Some people look their age only once in their life.

Sex speaks with forked tongue, don't you wish.

It is too much to require of intelligence that it be beautiful.

When someone's cup runneth over, someone else gets wet.

Pretentiousness is its own reward.

Men with obscure virtues are seldom as well known as those with obscure vices.

Expertise never comes in a small size.

It is reasonable to ask whether the trains will ever run on time. It is unreasonable to expect an answer.

Comfort is always bitter and small.

Being prepared for any emergency means keeping a good disguise handy.

The warning shot warns the shooter.

Evil is dark and shadowy in one dimension but life is dark and shadowy in three.

Imagination is not a dependable mode of transportation.

Undertakers believe in the angel of death.

Almost anything will stand on its own for a little while.

There is nothing like a little terror to make reality more real.

To grow old without growing wise is a bad thing. Worse is to grow wise without growing old. The absolute worst thing that can happen though, is not to grow old at all.

Someone else's memories make the best gossip.

Nothing in excess is excessive.

Reality can always become too real to be borne.

In sex as in life, there are no divisions worth a damn.

Some diseases know us better than we know ourselves.

There are some diseases even leeches can cure.

You can always enjoy youth, only not your own.

Some doctors cure bit by bit; others in one fell swoop.

The germ wishes it could cure a only it doesn't know how.

A person may be foolish only because he had lost, another only because he has won, and a third only because he has refused to play the game.

A man's reputation may hinge not on how he avoids, but how he recovers from, foolishness.

Death is nothing but terminal foolishness.

Some men are public fools, other practice their foolishness in private.

Every written book is a victory of sensibility over sense.

Every sentence is a jig saw puzzle with most of the pieces missing.

Not every word we read has been written.

The future always delivers less than it promises but more than we can handle.

Common sense is not a guide to great literature.

Irrationality is best served raw not cooked.

Things are forbidden only as a warning.

It is not good advice to forgive too much or forbid too little. In fact, it is not advice at all.

To the starving man there is only one kind of food.

A name is a habit existence develops but does not require.

Some people are paid by the minute for the hour, other are paid by the hour for the minute.

Some people work hardest when they are having fun.

Advertisements make promises that products can't keep.

We do not learn something when we discover it is true and forget it when it becomes false.

We may use any occasion to celebrate the death of a tyrant.

By definition, saints and kings are born on holy days.

It is unreasonable to be rational reaching for the moon.

It is unreasonable to insist on rationality where guessing will do.

Rationality is the guardian of illusion and stepfather of superstition.

Sometimes people want something just a instant after they need it, and they need something just a fraction of a second after they had it and let it go.

The best joke in the world is in the process of being told.

In the just society, permitting people to live out erroneous beliefs will be a criminal act.

Politics gives compromise a bad name.

Politics starts out as a necessity and ends up as a vice.

Like all perversions, politics makes pleasurable what most people find distasteful.

Rationality gets you in trouble; irrationality gets you in trouble; You are in trouble.

Life is a Punch and Judy show and you're the Judy.

Some people believe growing up is merely growing old with a vengeance.

Only a master craftsman can use a hammer of clay.

The human mind is the slide rule of tomorrow.

Kites designed to fly the highest don't require wind at all.

The one firm rule of creation is: solutions are created first. Problems are created only if the solutions do not work.

The Quotations of SG

Religion is a set of beliefs for those embarrassed by being human.

Babies are nature's way of explaining sex in exactly the same way in which fat is nature's way of explaining food.

Needing and wanting turn out to be the same thing about as often as the person you fall in love with turns out to be the person who falls in love with you.

Only human inefficiency makes human efficiency bearable.

Sex is like groping with your feet for something that you can not grasp with your hands.

We mourn in our victory the death of possibility.

It is nowhere written that you have to be happy with what pleases you most.

Some people require more to satisfy them than to make them happy.

Truth makes little effort to appear true. Lies try harder, they must be convincing.

Most people have two childhoods, one too early, one too late.

The best part of us always dies in some
childhood tragedy while the worst part of us
grows up with two sets of parents.

The trouble with men is that they think that
the same thing that caused a thing to happen
explains it. The trouble with women is that they
know that this is not so—and they know why.

There are three sides to any truth, one side
to obvious to be noticed, another to subtle
to be overlooked and a third to clear to be
understood.

Arguing that machines can't think because they
can't think like men is the same as arguing men
can't fly because they can't fly like birds.

Clever is what adults are when they think like
children.

Sophisticated means to be able to do something
before you know the name for what you are
doing and why you're doing it.

In matters of love, rub a thorn, remember the
knife.

An aroused and agitated creativity is one of
God's fiercer creatures.

Failure misuses us, victory uses us up.

It is almost impossible to locate the exact point at which the comic becomes tragic but it is the same point at which adolescence turns into middle age.

There is something about beauty that is repugnant to effort. At the same time, there is something about effort that makes it repugnant to beauty.

Beauty is always bait for one trap or another.

Looking back requires that one stop and turn around.

He was so loved that when he died no one would come forth to identify the body.

Many people think of surrendering but never find a general worth surrendering to.

A lost love is a lost life.

Any good idea is as translatable into theoretical physics as it is into a sonnet.

Only words travel by word of mouth: It takes art to move ideas.

There are certain hard cold facts, believing in which is equivalent to believing in the tooth fairy.

The devil works harder than God to achieve the same end. That's his punishment.

Pain is something for which everyone makes time.

Virtue is always unreasonable, vice never.

Unnatural virtue breeds contempt.

Scars breed: for instance a painter's scars breed art.

The capacity to sin is a potentially underdeveloped resource.

The real story of creation never appeared in the Bible for the simple reason that it is still going on.

Even rats and mice gossip.

Even God needs someone to keep score.

Most of us outgrow childhood: only the truly lucky ones outgrow adulthood.

Sex has many competitors as a vice, few as a virtue.

Sex is footnote to love.

Intuition lies frequently enough to be mistrusted.

Sex is man's only defense against ungodly desire.

Some people are saints only because they give their foolishness away with all of their other possessions.

Folly is one of those rare prizes that some people struggle to gain, others are given, and still others win in the lottery.

Folly's discipline is as exacting as wisdom's.

The worst fool flatters foolishness.

Foolishness has no ancestors only descendants.

It is possible to write sentences that hum with words that bark. This is what makes writing an art.

To a modern musician silence is not an inferior sound.

There are silences so profound even the deaf hear them.

Putting one foot in front of the other is not dancing, at least not dancing well.

In great writing there is always a struggle between words and sense that sense wins, almost, but only in the end.

Some people remind you of a sentence you have written, then forgotten, and then forgotten you have written, then forgotten you have forgotten.

A great novel is merely the concentration of the diffuse light that illuminates a thousand living rooms.

In a creative society the guardian of reason is the least rational being available.

Never measure the value of a question by the value of its answer.

Evolving is not traveling anywhere.

Men have one childhood, women two.

Imitating yourself does not produce good sex.

It is easier to live with the life you choose then the thousands of lives you choose not to live.

The only difference worth noticing between two saints is they way they dress.

Great writers write in order to find out what they have to say; less great writers because they want to hear themselves say it.

Art is what remains when all of the recognizable pieces of anything are taken away.

It is always easier to outrun the carrot than the stick. Never outrun the carrot:

There's a custom tailored logic for every madman.

Enthusiasm is a medium of exchange.

What we choose to forget is more important than what we care to remember.

Creativity is the willingness to plagiarize God.

No one goes to the trouble of destroying that which has no value.

Priest tells us what we should not want, parents what we shouldn't do, spouse tells us what we don't need, government what we can't have: No wonder we can't hear the voice inside that tells us what would make us happy.

Quotations from the BOCW Vol 1

Sometimes making a mistake that one knows is a mistake is a stupid thing to; sometimes it is an act of genius.

Mistakes are one of the most efficient means of gathering information – but a very dangerous one.

We hardly ever repeat our first mistake; our first mistake is almost always unique and unrepeatable because it comes from our innocence. Our second mistake though is reproducible without any effort at all and we make it, on the fly, in infinite variations.

Insisting that machines can't think because they can't think like men is like arguing men can't fly because they can't fly like birds.

Any really good mistake can be taught to a two year old. any really, really, good mistake can be built into a machine.

When information is plentiful and cheap intelligence is scarce and dear.

We may have a choice about which mistakes we make: we may not have a choice in which mistakes we perpetuate.

Mistakes are made only in retrospect – looking backward.
From the point at which we made it, looking forward, there
was only a choice.

For a computer a million microseconds makes a
second; for humans no such addition is possible.

No mistake is ever brought into the world an
orphan, alone, by itself. Mistakes always appear
in tuples and tuplets with parents and siblings.
And we bring them into the world already
reproducing, their progeny already growing.

A guess is the always available equivalent of
any finite amount of information and enough
information to take any action.

None of us mind making a mistake as long as we
can find an explanation, a good reason for having
made it, but for most of us, in a pinch, an excuse
will do.

The nature of a mistake becomes visible only
when we try to correct it.

How come we can see other peoples mistakes
before they make them and we cannot recognize
our own even after we see their consequences?

Only really big mistakes are made in good faith
and for good reasons.

The order in which mistakes are made is as important as the mistakes themselves. It is often easy to correct mistakes made in one order and nearly impossible to correct the same mistakes made in a different order.

The lack of control we have over our own lives is made absolutely clear by pointing out that we are unable to pick which of our flaws will be fatal.

We always live under the cloud of the mistakes of others and the consequences of the mistakes of the dead weigh heavily on us.

Most people would prefer to live with their first mistake rather than their second. On the other hand most people would prefer to be buried with their second than their first.

Some information is impossible to get; it doesn't exist at all until you try to get it and doesn't survive the attempt to extract it.

Every wedding usually breaks into two sides; those who think the bride is making a horrible blunder and those who think the groom is making a fatal mistake. This is not the same set of sides as those who think the bride is getting the best of the bargain as opposed to those who believe the groom is getting the best deal, and these are both different from the side that believes the divorce will be amicable and the side that is convinced the divorce will be contentious.

The first mistake we make in the world is believing that our achievements are a product of our intelligence and effort and insight into the world. The second mistake we make is that we forget that this is a mistake.

In the end it is only our mistakes that make sense of the world and it is only the mistakes that we are comfortable with that make life worth living – in fact, that that make living possible at all.

More than a few people make their careers in the world counterfeiting other people's mistakes.

The first mistake we make we are likely to make on our own; after that we never make a mistake on our own again. We always get help.

Significant variations of any doctrine, particularly the heresies a doctrine gives birth to, are part of the doctrine. There are only so many significant variations to any doctrine and these are essential parts of the doctrine.

It is nearly impossible for a person to make more than one really fatal mistake; but a few people, by persistence and determination are able to pull it off.

There are no virgin mistakes. Every mistake you make has been made by many people, many times before you.

Imitating their mistakes is probably the greatest compliment we can pay someone we love.

We all make our first big mistake by accident. Our second mistake is almost always an attempt to correct the first mistake. The third mistake is an attempt to mitigate the effects of the second and the fourth to control the damage the third produced. Very few of us quit while we are ahead of the game.

The first big mistake he made he could have avoided but did not. The second big mistake could have avoided him but did not.

The front end of every mistake is different; the back end is always the same.

Our mistakes get harder to correct as we get more practice in making them.

Mistakes are measures of something – but of what is never clear.

Nature's mistakes become instantly part of our common nature and the root of many of the unique mistakes we make.

We learn most about ourselves from other people's mistakes. We often fail to learn much from our own mistakes.

There are two kinds of mistakes; those that can be corrected by persistence and effort and those which persistence and effort makes worse. But given any particular mistake it is never possible to tell which kind it is.

Often, people's mistakes may be corrected by pointing out to them they are mistakes. For some people this does not work.

Often we don't have enough information to make the correct mistakes. Whenever something exists it carries information, unfortunately often just not the information we need or can use.

No one ever became famous for the second big mistake they made.

What makes a mistake a really tragic mistake is often a matter of timing and bad taste.

Evolution may be nature's big mistake. It is enormously wasteful and takes recycling one step to far.

Many mistakes are anonymous.

We hardly ever choose to repeat our second mistake. The third is always anathema to us; the fourth we remember and its lessons are seared into our brain. The fifth one we can repeat from memory and avoid like the plague. But we never fall out of love with our first mistake.

*Our first mistake is usally beautiful, arouses our desire, but usu-
ally something we really cannot afford. Our second mistake is
usually quite common but cheap – and we can get it on credit.*

The basis for calling a statement a lie is hardly
ever that it does not correspond to reality; a lie
consists of the intent to deceive. But sometimes
the intent to deceive comes close to being a lie
itself.

Some people become better people trying to
approximate the lies they tell about themselves.

People who lie at random are often believed at
random also.

Over the course of a lifetime childhood lies
harden into some-thing stronger than concrete
and become the foundation on which a strong
person builds her middle years and old age.

Sometime the habit of telling lies is so
ingrained that telling truth seems like speaking
a foreign language.

As the truth about the world becomes more
complicated and more difficult to understand,
the lies about the world become simpler and
easier to believe.

A lie may consist only in the order in which a
set of truths are put together.

What makes some lies particularly contemptible and egregious is that no one benefits from their telling.

When to lie and what to lie about and to whom to lie are the most difficult problems children have to solve before they can become adults and many of our problems as adults stem from not having solved this problem well.

Sometimes a lie is a perspective on the truth that we are just unable to take. A lie is often a view of something that is true but from an impossibly obtuse angle.

Put the head where the tail should be, and the tail where the head should be and the animal is more or less the same – almost.

An overly sincere compliment, told energetically may be as close to a lie as an honest man can get.

When they break, lies fracture into smaller pieces than truths and any collection of truths will fit into a smaller space than any collection of lies.

Lies often forget who told them but always remember those who believed them.

It is easier to swim in an ocean of truths than float in a lake of lies.

Chewing on a lie is like chewing on a bone that made of the same stuff that teeth are made of.

If the truth bled like a person when they were nicked being shaved we would all be better off a little.

Some people who are incapable of telling other people a lie are incapable of telling themselves the truth.

It is not only individuals who lie. Generations, corporations, whole classes of people are capable of lying. Nations often are prodigious liars; most are incapable of telling the truth to themselves as a people or to other countries.

Animals find it difficult to lie: occasionally, when really hard pressed, they will simulate a lie and will pretend to be some other animal out of embarrassment.

Some great liars have weak stomachs and confess their lies almost the instant they make them. Those to whom they have lied must un-believe something so quickly it makes them sea sick.

Lies collapse from the edge inward, truth always from the center out.

A lie is always stretching for the truth that it cannot quite reach and cannot grasp when it reaches it.

When it comes to believing in the unbelievable we often cheat.
Pyramids and Hierarchies of beliefs are often upside down.
The least believable thing is on the bottom.

A lie lives between a reality that common
sense and intelligence is forced to believe and a
desire that refuses to believe it.

There's a musicality to speaking; telling the
truth then lying is different from lying then
telling the truth; telling two lies in a row is
quite different than alternating a truth and a lie,
or telling two truths in a row. The best liars are
good at lying because they have mastered the
rhythm of lying.

Many unintelligible actions of people
are attempts to avoid having told a lie, by
struggling, after the fact, to make reality
approximate what the lie said it was.

Lies are assemblages of pieces that do not
naturally make up what they are asserted they
make up. The smallest pieces of any lie may be
true. The lie consists of their assemblage, the
way they are put together not the falsity of any
particular part.

Between any two pieces of common sense reality
there is something nearly impossible to believe.

Each of us wants to believe in at least one unbelievable thing. For some this is a statement about desire; for others it is a proposition of logic.

Unbelievable is very different than impossible.

You can move from the absolutely undeniable to the unbelievable in one small step or one great leap. But the distance moved is the same.

We all want to believe in some things that reality will not let us believe in. A lie closes the gap between what we want to believe and reality. A lie lives between a reality that common sense and intelligence is forced to believe and a fluid desire that refuses to believe it.

The virtuous whore is the invention of the virtuous pimp.

Life is littered with fissures, chasms, abysses: an illusion often bridges these voids.

When nature makes something look like something it takes pains to make it act like that thing also.

When there is nothing left to remember there is almost nothing to look forward to.

An illusion often feels more real than the reality it distorts. We are often forced to accept a reality; we usually embrace an illusion willingly.

*Like Pinocchio, the very best illusions have the capacity to be-
come real.*

Most illusions are self-cleaning, self-
maintaining, and self-repairing.

Some people covet other people's illusions. Few
illusions are completely technical.

Many people demand an illusion when a
simple mistake will do.

Packing all of a society's illusions into religion is
an interesting maneuver which mostly does not
work.

Nature makes progress by increasing the
distance between any reality and its illusions;
man makes progress by decreasing it.

It is difficult to identify any step forward that
does not begin with an illusion.

Nature never builds anything that cannot serve
both as a reality and an illusion.

It looked like love at first sight but only until
he opened his eyes.

Most people demand reality but will settle for a
good illusion.

Things that look far away are far away. Things that look close by are close by. Most of us know that this is an illusion but we believe it anyway.

Most people do not mind sharing their illusions but sharing their reality is too much.

Beware nature pretending.

In any democracy the people are the illusion.

The asymptote of any illusion is a different illusion.

Most successful, common sense, utilitarian objects have at least one illusion as a working, central part.

It is easy to refuse to believe that something is an illusion; it is usually very difficult to prove.

Illusions most often maintain distance between things that are very close in reality.

A society is defined by the illusions to which it clings.

We refuse to recognize some illusions out of politeness, others out of hubris, still others out of habit.

There are illusions that amount treason, but most just amount to surrender.

Sometimes you can tell something is an illusion but you cannot tell what it is an illusion of.

Most illusions are symmetric about only one point.

Many illusions are merely technical, others merely practical, some a matter of honor.

It is a major error to cling to the last generation's illusions.

Illusions and realities often come in pairs.

An illusion may kill with real weapons or imagined weapons:

Illusions linger on reality like the smell of an extraordinarily expensive perfume, a reminder of something that was there just a moment ago but has disappeared forever.

Time is a less than zero sum game.

The order of a good family is more like the order of a shipwreck than a corporation.

The world ought to make it immediately clear when one order has changed into a different order, but it almost never does. Most significant changes from one kind of system into another kind of system are disguised as insignificant changes from one system to a minor variation of it.

The most important detail in any system of control is from what part it leaks.

It's hard to tell when an order is tilting and even
more difficult to tell when it is leaning too far
and will fall and crush you.

The sequence of steps that create an order
from disorder or transform one order into a
different order is never clear, either what the
steps actually are, or what the steps are between.

Order always has a head and a tail and a
shadow. The shadow does show the tail however.

Running away to escape nearly always fails
because of a poor sense of direction and a bad
sense of distance.

You can always borrow against any order.
Every order has money in the bank. But often
not in small denominations or in the currency
you would like.

There are quite a few simulations of order that
do not bring order into existence.

A bad order is one step away from chaos; a
good order is one step away from no order at all.

There are orders you can lean against and
orders you can leap on and some orders that are
fragile beyond belief.

Some small orders can be enlarged into big orders and some big orders can be reduced to small orders. But this is not always true of all orders and it is not clear why.

Some people find order where others find merely boring, meaningless repetition.

When you perfectly counterfeit order you seldom get a genuine order.

Sometimes chaos is a strategy, sometimes it is a diversion, other times it is a distraction. Most times it is a nuisance.

Judging two systems as similar because they have similar organizational charts may be like judging two women as similar on the basis of the fact that they have the same bra size, use the same perfume, or have the same lover.

Often the starting point of any motion is not the place you begin the moving from. Nor is where you stop the place where motion ceases.

One of the few inalienable rights government takes from us is our ability to choose which disorder we shall live under. This makes the perpetual question in any democracy how much of what order do we have to accept and participate in to be free.

Innovation is sometimes a matter of poor memory.

A good order is closer to no order than to a rigid order.

Some individuals mimic order to bring order
into their lives; some individuals mimic order
to bring disorder into their lives. Either strategy
will work but people still recognize them as
mimics.

It is easy to mistake chaos for the absence of
order; it is easy to mistake disorder for chaos.

Sometimes chaos is a strategy for bringing
order into a situation.

It is the nature of order that it is invisible; it is in
the nature of disorder that it is not.

What counts as new depends on how old
you are and how old you were when the last
newness happened.

Every significant organ of the body creates its
own order and its own sense of order.

A political philosophy is a matter of believing
which and how much of the population are
dispensable and how they should be dispensed.

There is no line which can circumscribe a good
order, no geometric figure which can give it
form.

Two points give you a space for betweenness but it takes three to give you a between. Every significant innovation is a between with only one end of its betweenness visible.

Holding on to what you have often means gripping tightly what you are certain to lose instead of grabbing for something you are not likely to get.

Being partially visible is not the same thing as being partially invisible.

There are as many things disinvented as invented.

It is nowhere written that have to be happy with what satisfies you most.

The rich and powerful are distinguished from the rest of us by being able to have other people work to satisfy their desires but prevent them, like cormorants, from enjoying their satisfaction.

Desires bind us to people that wants would not and needs cannot, people we would prefer not to be bound to.

We have not yet figured out how taking need out of the human equation changes the human equation.

Win or lose, there is no game more frustrating or more satisfying than the game of desire. When it is played well, the game of desire does not even require players, only an audience. This is true even if, in most cases, the players are the audience.

Some religions shape desire; some pay more attention to shaping how desire is satisfied, although why either should matter to God is a mystery.

Every religion promises man shall not want for desire only satisfaction. We all could probably use a religion that promised fewer desires and more satisfaction.

For some of us desire is a privilege we are denied because of our social standing. This is wrong. The frustration of desire is the unalienable right of every human being.

We are, most of us, often and unfortunately, only the caretakers of someone else's desires.

The only thing that survives our death is way in which we satisfied our desires.

The difference between high quality and low quality desires is artificial and manufactured – an illusion. The difference between high quality satisfaction and low quality satisfaction of any desire however, is as real as anything can get.

It is important to distinguish what you need from what you want. It is even more important to distinguish what you want from what you want to want. But what is most important is to distinguish what you want badly from what you want badly but not badly enough.

The list of complaints about desire is small;
Frustration, disappointment – occasionally a lost
or borrowed or stolen identity.

Some of our illnesses are side effects of our
desires. Very few are side effects of needs.

Sometimes we recognize as person only as the
image of a desire we had a long time ago.

Every desire lies to the person who has it about
the object he has it about.

The geometry of want, the arithmetic of need,
the topology of desire, exhaust the mathematics
of human existence.

Some people pride themselves that their desires
are always incomplete.

'Cannot' has never killed off a desire, nor
'should not' finished off a want.

The least exciting pornography in the world is
watching desire reproduce.

Forgotten desires are often more powerful than
remembered desires.

One forgets a need as soon as it is satisfied; one never forgets a satisfied desire.

Some people are defined by the way they remember desire. Others the way they forget needs.

Needs are democratic; wants are not.

Desires that are satisfied too quickly are hardly satisfied at all. Needs that are satisfied at all are never satisfied quickly enough.

Some things make a complete circuit; they start out as needs, develop into wants, and grow into desire. For others the path is completely opposite. It is a question whether you can call this figure a circle.

Some desires have no future; others have no past.

That nature would keep us from being able to meddle and muck around with our needs is sensible. On the other hand not giving us control over or even access to our desires was just spiteful.

Every great portrait that has ever been painted is great precisely because it displays, in some inscrutable and incomprehensible but absolutely tangible and obvious way, the character of the sitters wants and desires.

The man is cursed who outlives his desires.

Needs link us to the past; desires and wants link us to the future.

The man for whom needs wants and desires are merely different names for the same thing is blessed and very rare.

We die in stages; first desire withers, then wants dry up ; finally needs diminish slightly – and poof.

We can reconstruct the whole of any desire from the smallest sliver of a fragment of a piece.

We know some of the most intimate aspects of our lives obliquely and indirectly, our needs, wants and desires for example. We only know them through the things that satisfy them and make them go away.

When the fire of desire goes out we would warm ourselves by the ashes except the ash of desire has the smell of burnt flesh.

What God really wanted to prohibit he made it impossible to desire.

The impulse driving us to become born again often comes from the wish to have ones desires reborn.

Human beings, the species Homo Sapiens, may only be an ex-periment, nature's way of testing out the hypothesis that life can be organized by need, want and desire.

Ghosts are just the accumulated residue of dead person's un-fulfilled desire.

Science hides the really important pieces of knowledge in plain sight; it disguises them as hypotheses and findings and theories, buries them in abstracts and journal papers so that we can never be clear about them. Most of all it camouflages them with doubt.

Science is best conceived as (and works best when it is) a dialogue with nature in which nature does most of the talking.

Science hardly ever lights the world where the world is really dark. Science only goes where the world is always already lit up.

Science is a mirror in which man sees a distorted image of himself, distorted.

To think of science as other than a human activity is wrong; to think of science as only a human activity is even more wrong. But it is not clear in what the error consists or how to correct it.

Science is a machine with a working accelerator but a broke brake.

What it cannot understand science misinterprets.

Understanding the limits of science is not a scientific pursuit.

The effectiveness of science falls off the nearer to the human domain it comes.

The dialog between science and art is the dialog between the imagination of the head and the imagination of the heart.

Science is not a single thing. To the chemist, science is chemistry; to the physicist, science is physics; to the biologist, science is biology. To call science a single thing is certainly unscientific and dead wrong.

Science reflects our weaknesses as well as our strengths, but reflects one of them better than the other – but we cannot tell which.

New sciences appear and disappear without anyone noticing.

Much of our trouble with science comes from the fact that we are trying to control it as if it were a pubescent girl rather than a musth crazed elephant. The rest of the trouble with science happens because science evolves at a different rate and in a different way than human beings.

Science is always a compromise between our demand that things be explained and our demand to have them explained in a way we can understand. There is always the possibility that in at least one particular case we will not be able to understand science's explanation of something.

Science rarely speaks to us in the language of science and when it does we do not hear it.

There are some things science is not and does not want to be but which it is forced to be again and again.

Trivial is not a scientific judgment.

By the time science is ready to celebrate the joy is already out of the reason for the celebration.

Science is always involved in forcing the world into a mold. Its virtue is that the mold is always changing.

Science is a compromise between our need to know the world and the world's insistence on being known.

Science comes in two forms; swift and bitter; slow and sour;

Sweet and lingering is not in its vocabulary

Technology is science on steroids and stilts.

Science is an activity man carries on always in partnership with machines.

Nature finds itself powerless to resist the demands of scientific inquiry. Only human beings are strong enough and stupid enough to resist the application of science.

Science is modern economics in drag. What this means to say is that science, like economics does a considerable part of its work by smashing, pounding, and destroying; its major accomplishments come infrequently but consist of setting itself ablaze, pushing the ashes aside and settling into the space it has created.

People are always asking what they would find if people turned science on itself. But they do not really want to know.

Every time and place gets more and better art than it deserves; the excess is for the rest of us who come later, after it.

It is not clear what art for a cat or for a dog or for a tiger would be; in fact, it is pretty obvious they do not have art at all. Nevertheless, it is a productive and wonderful exercise for any artist to make art for dogs or cats or tigers.

Good works of art do not present themselves as completed and finished objects. The best works of art present themselves as an incomplete project ready for you to complete. And the very best works of art come with the tools you need to complete it.

'Art' appears only when we write or talk about art. Otherwise there are only people struggling, people busy making things, doing things, buying and selling things.

Some people aspire to be a work of art but the work necessary to achieve it is too onerous.

Art is sometimes little more than a placeholder, a marker which identifies a location to the right or left of a wave in the ocean, somewhere above or below some grain of sand in a desert.

Most people think art works directly on our senses. Actually art bypasses the senses and goes exactly to the places where the senses go, and further than the senses can take you.

Art is what remains when the recognizable parts of anything are taken away.

Art lives in the crevices, on the edges and ends of the world; at the worst on a dead end street on a deserted island; at best, in the back yard of a foreclosed house next to a child's swing.

Art is the place where things start and the place where things end. We squeeze the rest of living between them.

Art is always an unbalancing; the danger of art is that it unbalances things that it took a long time and a lot of effort to line up and stack on one another, things that are absolutely essential to be balanced in order to walk down the street and get lunch.

Art is always unbalancing; life is always rebalancing.

The exact same piece of art sometimes appears at different times, in different places, in a number of different materials, in a number of different forms.

Art is mankind stripped naked and made presentable.

Art is always recognizable instantaneously but only for an instant.

Art is the imitation of an echo of silence, the afterimage of an imagined image.

Art is less an object and more an attitude, a way of viciously attacking anything that cannot shake itself free from the bondage of existence and defend itself.

There is nothing that cannot be improved by being made into a work of art, which means perhaps, that there is nothing that cannot be made into a work of art except another work of art.

Art always makes itself both the figure and the ground. It does this by expanding the space that always exists between things.

Art is always motion stopped at exactly the place where movement has stopped. To go further would be fruitless and not get you anywhere.

Art always happens when a grip is loosened, when something is grasped as it is let go.

There can be no art on an empty stomach. For most of us art is art only on an overfilled stomach; for some people it is their entire diet but these are thin and sickly types.

Art continually makes judgments that are difficult even for artists to justify; it confuses itself as often as it confuses us.

A work of art is completely defined by what it leaves out, its complement, but its complement always exists in one more dimension than the work itself. Art can always be recognized by how it changes the objects around it.

Art is easily confused but it is not easily distracted.

There is nothing that someone, somewhere cannot pass off, intelligently and sincerely, as a work of art.

Art is a piece of clothing that is not wearable, a chunk of food that is not edible, always something that denies its being.

Some people attempt to commit suicide by drowning themselves in pleasure; it is almost always only a cry for help.

It is the curse of love that often we need from someone we love exactly that thing that they are incapable of providing regardless of how much they want to. This is not true of friendship which, when it is well founded, links two people who need from one another exactly what is most natural for each to effortlessly and freely give.

Pleasures may be embellished, embroidered, and decorated out of all reason and any sense of taste.

A particular pleasure once a month is one thing. The same pleasure once a day is another. Exactly the same pleasure six times an hour is another thing entirely.

It is in the way he pursues pleasure rather than the way he avoids pain that distinguishes man from other animals. And it is in the way they discriminate different kinds of pleasure that people differ most.

To honor a man you must first honor his pleasures; to honor a woman you must first honor her pains.

To make sense out of human pleasures they must be mathematically treated, scaled and topologically transformed. When one does this one recognizes that pleasures have been and are a constant in human life.

Evolution has not changed pleasure only made it more appropriate to the seasons.

Pleasures have feathers and hair and opposable thumbs and hoofs and scales and sharp tongues.

What a culture identifies as pleasure and the way it enjoys those pleasures define a culture.

For some people it is a pleasure to be caught between a rock and a hard place;

Do computers get their pleasure from electricity or information? It is hard to say. What is certain is that there will be no artificial intelligence until there is artificial pleasure.

Pleasure is always simultaneously a debt paid and a debt assumed.

In old age a man may still pursue childish pleasures.

With pleasure timing is everything; a moment too soon, a minute to late and goodbye pleasure.

Pleasure and politics both require negotiating a balance between freedom and constraint – but quite a different balance.

Pleasure which cannot be enjoyed must be endured. There is no escaping pleasure no matter how hard you try.

The roots of pleasure are deep and they hold it firm and steady, roots up, in the air.

Pleasure and pain are not a zero sum game. Reducing pain is not the same as increasing pleasure. And certainly increasing pleasure does not mean decreasing pain.

People often make pleasure into a tool. Some shape it into a compass to find their way in the world; others form it into a hammer to beat themselves and others into submission

A saint is a man who is willing to share his pleasures with you without demanding that you share his pain but has no pleasures to share.

The presence of pain is not a higher moral state than the absence of pleasure; it only seems that way.

Learning to desire odd pleasures takes a considerable amount of practice and skill. And odd pleasures require considerable tact and intrapersonal skill to come to terms with owning them. The very oddest ones take more effort coming to terms with having than satisfying

There is the quality of pleasure and the duration of pleasure and the quantity of pleasure. There should be an economics of pleasure – and there is. What makes it strange is that the economics of pleasure is more like the economics of agriculture rather than the economics of manufacturing.

There are different exchange systems in the economics of pleasure. Money may change hands, but mostly pleasure is bartered– sometimes for pleasure, sometimes for something else.

When it comes to pleasure accidents are as valuable as good planning.

It is as possible to be clumsy when it comes to pleasure as it is to be elegant and refined; what makes it pleasure is that it doesn't make a difference.

Every human hook is baited with pleasure; which pleasure depends on what one is fishing for.

Pleasures never have the same father and always have different mothers but they are all related and all of them share a family resemblance.

As we get old, pleasure abandons us and returns back home. Unfortunately this usually happens before we do, while we can still miss it.

It is sometimes hard to tell if pleasure is the compensation or the reward for loving.

Everyday life tames thought, sometimes the way humans break a horse – by riding it until its spirit is broken – sometimes the way the earth tames a river – by giving it mountains to run through and a sea to run into.

We often judge the rationality of a person's actions by their consequences rather than the nature of the thought that led to them. Unfortunately this makes power the ultimate arbiter of reason and rationality.

If we could feel how we think it would save us from many mistakes although feeling being rational would embarrass half of us and make the other half giggly.

Sense and rationality provide the best demonstration of the limits of our reason. Rationality often takes us to a place where rationality is of no use at all.

When being reasonable turned into being rational is hard to tell; earlier than yesterday certainly, but probably no later than last week.

Between thinking rationally about the world and thinking reasonably about the world is a gap that thought cannot bridge.

The world meets thought half way, but only halfway, and unfortunately the wrong half.

Thinking always requires a space in which the thinking can take place. The first task of thinking is creating a space in which thinking can take place. The second task of thinking is not to get lost in that space.

Rational thought is rational only half of the time; what is rational the other half of the time is unreasonable, irrational and inopportune.

It is almost never the case that thinking can get us out of trouble that thinking has gotten us into.

What we call common sense is the least common thing about us.

It does not make sense to be reasonable reaching for the moon.

Sense cannot make of the world something that it is not even though it wants to be desperately.

Like its pains, the rationalities of all historical ages are pretty much the same. No age is remembered by its rationalities. Every historical age is remembered by those of its irrationalities that are distinct and distinctive.

There is no project however reasonable that cannot be made irrational by the addition of one other additional reasonable element.

We try to avoid making mistakes by being rational but being rational does not guarantee that mistakes will not be made.

Thinking is a crutch for doing. At the same time doing is a crutch for thinking. We are always hobbling our way through the world bouncing from one crutch to the other.

We can only make sense out of things that are at a distance from and external to us. This is especially true for those things that are an intimate part of us. We are constantly forced to push parts of ourselves away from us in order to understand them.

Skip a single link of any chain of rational actions and the whole chain seems crazy and falls apart.

We often get lost because we have no good map of our pleasures.

Things and people make a lot of sense to us when they are ir-rational and unreasonable. We have an absolutely firm grasp instantly on what is going on when a person goes crazy.

We are reasonable and rational only because we are backed up against a wall and have no choice – and because we lack the resources to be irrational and unreasonable

Unfortunately to humans the world is not reasonable or sensible in our understanding of reason and sense. Behaving rationally may be irrational; just as behaving irrationally may be an exquisitely rational act.

Sense, especially of the common sort, is an adornment the world often wears as bait.

Familiarity makes almost anything reasonable and habit defines reason for most of us.

We do not abandon a way of thinking just because it is proved wrong; nor do we accept a way of thinking just because it comes to provably correct conclusions. There are matters of taste and judgment involved.

Thought is usually applied to the problem of closing of distance rather than opening it up.

None of our parent's rationalities ever strikes us as particularly rational.

Reason grows not by extending its reach and making irrational things more rational; rationality grows by squeezing more irrationalities between rationalities, hiding them and making them harder to see.

Being reasonable and rational consists of more than not being unreasonable and not being irrational – but not much more.

It may be that change, besides being unpredictable, is vicious.

Adding chance, a piece at a time, without stopping, does not create chaos. Nor does removing chance, forever, one piece at a time create order. Why this is so no one knows.

The point in a system in which chance appears is as important as the point in a system where order disappears – but it is never the same point.

We ourselves often change ourselves without our permission. Death is just the coming together of all of the elements of randomness in a person's life, at the same time, in the same place—often by accident.

The nature of the order we find in the world is revealed by the kind of chance we discover in it.

Chance squeezes order out of the world the way humans squeeze blood from a stone; it just does not let go.

The familiar elements of chance are essential elements of any well-worn order.

A good definition of chance should not only
exhibit its meaning but show how it looks to us
when we are tired or drunk or half asleep.

Approach a point from one direction you reach a chaos;
approach exactly the same point from another direction
you reach a perfect order This is as good a definition of
chance as you are likely to get.

Chance is a matter of perspective; roulette
for instance. On any given spin whether your
number will win is a matter of chance; over all
possible spins the chance the house will win is
certain.

Pleasure requires at least some discipline
and practice; pain comes even if you are
completely impulsive and disorganized and
whether you practice or not.

Chance and change are great teachers. They have
nothing at all to say about right and wrong. They
teach us to be quick footed and cautious about
taking the world for granted; and they urge us to
be flexible, really flexible.

Change never lies; chance hardly ever tells the
truth.

It is to the world's credit that it tolerates any order at all.
There are as many orders in the world as there are 'nexts' in the
world, and as many chances in the world as there are 'befores.'

Chance is a vicious school yard bully and order
is an innocent, virtuous, virginal girl; so much
for the mythos of science.

Even change changes, often by chance.

Different kinds of chance exist in the world; the
reason we do not see them is that we always see
them as just deviations from order.

Some things completely disappear when the
chance elements in them are removed. Other
things change completely when the chance
elements of them are replaced by other chance
elements.

The iron test of our intimate relationship with
chance is that we recognize chance no matter
what form it takes the way we recognize a
person no matter what hat they put on.

Chance inserts itself in order in ways we cannot
understand.

Identifying clearly seven deadly sins give most
of us a chance at what otherwise would be an
impossibly fast moving target.

If we had to construct a list of seven deadly sins on our own, most of us would start repeating ourselves at four give or take two.

Chance and change teach us not only that the map is not the territory but that what we take to be the map may not even be a map.

Sloppiness approximates randomness only to the extent that habits approximate order.

Randomness exposes our dependence on devices and machines. Redundancy mocks our attempts at randomness.

We try to balance some parts of our lives by adding a bit of chance and other parts by adding a little bit of order but we hardly ever get the balance right.

Each of us believes in our heart that we can do a better job of improving the world than chance and change. And we are probably right. But there are just too many of us.

We look at the stars and, except for the astronomers among us, we see something unchanging and eternal; but chance and change stare back at us; The same is true when we look at a mountain or the ocean; we see things immutable and enduring– until an earthquake or tsunami hits.

Someone always win the lottery but it is never you or me.

The lottery is the last chance at education
in any country in which the schools are going
down the tubes.

Sometimes we change the world out of
boredom, sometimes out of exuberance; but
often the world just changes itself because we
are distracted or have forgotten what it would
take to prevent the change.

We can change something directly by just
changing it; or we can change it by leaving
it the same and changing everything that is
connected to it. The result is only occasionally
the same.

One effective way of changing the world
is changing how you remember it. A more
effective way of changing the world is
changing the way other people remember it.

Chance and change are not necessarily
connected to one another in principle, only
in practice because when things change what
we experience most sharply are the chance
elements. For human beings unexpected
consequences are a way of life, a habit life has.

We cannot recognize chance and changes at anything but the human scale. In the very small and the very large chance and change escape us.

Change and chance: connected up, a ladder with no rungs; connected down, a swing with no seat.

At no point is any order symmetrical: no order is symmetrical at any point.

Many things camouflage themselves with chance to avoid detection.

Quotations from the BOCW Vol 2

Every order consists of a fractious, badly disciplined, and only partially controlled invisible organization of sub orders. When an order collapses its sub orders take control. If these collapse the smaller orders that make them up take control and if these collapse the sub orders that make them up take control. Completely rooting out an order is nearly impossible.

Order clings.

Every order harbors its own particular chaos.

Somethings are permanently partial and incomplete.

There is no separation between any two chaos'.

Order appears different depending on the direction and angle from which you look at it. What defines chaos is that it looks the same from whatever direction or angle you see it.

Chaos does not come in pieces. Nor can it be broken up into smaller parts. Chaos cannot crack or split or break apart, only melt.

Chaos is recognizable by any of the senses.

Every chaos is made to measure, by hand, to a particular set of measurements.

A standing army is an invitation to chaos.

We hardly ever confront chaos. Our own chaos is invisible to us and other people's chaos appears as the tiniest order it contain.

Chaos is nearly impossible to remember clearly but nearly impossible to forget.

Order always seeps into chaos in a different way than chaos seeps into order.

Chaos makes you yearn for disaster.

There is chaos in the large —and then there is the tiny chaos that rests in an infants hand.

The easiest way to produce chaos is to collect a number of exquisitely well put together orders.

You cannot protect your most precious possessions from chaos. You worthless possessions are safe however.

Random is different from disorder which is different from chaos but no one can tell you what the difference is.

Hardly anyone's education begins with learning the difference between randomness and disorder and chaos. Most people's education end when they learn the distinction.

Once an idea becomes scientific, once an idea is incorporat-
ed into some science or other it is lost to the rest of humanity
forever.

Meaning covers everything to an infinite depth.

All action is asymmetric.

Failure is sometimes merely the lack of success,
but sometimes it is much more.

Some people always see the symmetry of
success. The successful hardly ever see it.

Any chaos is as complete as it ever going to be.

It is surprising how delicate chaos really is.

Sometimes we see the connections between
things but not the things they connect.
Sometimes we see the things connected but not
the connections between them. Occasionally if
we are lucky we see them both.

What we want is to be whole. What we are is
connected.

Sometimes the connection between two things
is a bridge; sometimes it just the river flowing
under the bridge.

Sometimes the hardest connections to grasp are
the connections between a thing and itself.

Often it is possible to see a problem and see the solution to the problem but not the connection between them.

Connections age differently than the things they connect: sometimes quicker, sometimes slower.

Connections which were made in one way have to be sustained in another.

All connections depend on some technology, but the most complex ones on the simplest technologies.

Every technology produces new connections between things which invisibly re–create the things they connect.

The network of connections always overwhelms the connections that make it up.

You can't tell a connection by its appearance. Sometimes connections disguise themselves and masquerade as other connections completely.

Connections breed; sometimes this is a matter of economics, sometimes of biology. Often it is just because they can.

Often the value of one connection in a chain of connections is worth more than the whole chain.

Some connections are real, some imaginary. Sometimes the difference is no difference at all. The imaginary ones are often stronger than the real ones. We are constantly replacing real connections with imaginary ones which become real. Sometimes a connection is a mistake; sometimes a mistake is the connection.

Sometimes connections which are hard to break are easily misplaced.

Any collection of connections is incomplete. To complete them you have to add more connections.

All connections are incomplete but different connections are incomplete in different ways.

Some connections may be knitted or woven or knotted together; others may only be tangled.

Sometime we recognize a separation by what fills it and then only after the separation has disappeared.

Sometimes a separation is clear though what is separated from what is foggy.

A separation has to be created then maintained. Often the creation is easy, maintaining it may be difficult, and sometimes the person who creates it is not the person who has to maintain it.

A separation is defined by what it keeps from being connected.

The parts you use when you put something
together are not the parts you get when you take
the thing apart;

There are gaps that can be filled by putting stuff
in; there are gaps which can be filled by taking
stuff out.

Its size is not a good measure of a gap.

Sometimes the only way that you can identify a
gap is by what fills it.

There are no gaps in the infinite.

Some people's lives consist entirely of filling the
same gap over and over again, other people's
lives are filled with creating the same gap again
and again.

Some gaps are made of the same stuff they are
gaps in.

Some gaps are made of the same material they
are gaps in.

First we want closure, then continuity but in the
end we will settle for a small gap, a gap smaller
than our foot.

A gap can only be grasped by its middle.

The way you see the gaps in a person is to see where they leak from.

Some separations begin at the top and go to the bottom. Others grow from side to side.

What material a separation consists of is difficult to conceive.

Separations are not profiles of the things they separate.

Sometimes you cling to the separation as the only part of a person you can grasp, the only part of them that you can hold onto.

Sometimes when you push on a separation it disappears; sometimes it makes you disappear.

A single similarity may bridge and eliminate a multitude of differences.

Differences are assembled and constructed, and often, if not carefully maintained, disappear.

There are gaps that can be filled by putting stuff in; there are gaps which can be filled by taking stuff out.

Not every gap is an opportunity to get rid of your trash.

A distinction must be mounted and polished before it becomes a difference but if you embellish and elaborate a difference too much it disappears.

The separation created by a difference does not depend on the size of the difference.

A difference may make two different things the same.

Some gaps are indefinite, amorphous and uncertain. Others are definite, well-formed and sure.

Every next gives you a gap, which can be filled by another next, which give you another gap, sometimes the same gap, sometimes a different one..

The gaps between words are often not the same things as the gaps in the things the words are about.

Many people construct a life by collecting gaps and patching them together.

The center of a circle is not a gap.

Friends respect one another's gaps; lovers cannot abide them.

The first attack on a gap is an explanation.

Some gaps give birth to unexpected things.

A thing is really crazy when it is impossible to adjust the world around it to make it sensible and sane.

Sometimes a gap is a product of creative perception sometimes the complete failure of any perception at all.

To make a place at the table for crazies is a good thing. Putting them at the head of the table or in charge of the menu and service, food and silverware man not be so sensible.

A thing is absolutely crazy when it is impossible to adjust the world around it to make it sensible and sane. Something is really crazy when you cannot adjust the world around it to make it sensible and sane.

A point at which anything is (im)balanced but which cannot be adjusted produces madness.

The point at which words run out of meaning is a good measure of the quality of a writer and his writing.

There is a poverty of madness that arises when you are too poor to own the resources that would make you can appear sane.

Being sane and appearing sane are two different things.

The casually mad and the seriously mad are two different species.

A medicine that cures madness could also probably cure sanity but will hardly ever be used to do so.

Madness must be entertained and tolerated. It is the cost of doing business in the modern world.

The struggle with sanity is as heroic, virtuous and unfathomable an activity as any in the world.

What is the opposite of madness or insanity; it cannot be sanity because much sanity drives us into madness and into doing crazy things. it is certainly not intelligence; Intelligence and acuity is not the antithesis or opposite of madness. The polar opposite of insanity is another, different insanity.

Creating a measuring rod which one can use to plot distances from sanity is a impossible task.

Craziness may consist of a great clarity as well as a great confusion.

Only the very rich own the instruments for the manufacture of their own and others sanity.

Being sane and appearing sane are two different things.

The truly random applied in any real domain will generate madness.

Some generals organize their armies as kindergarten classes; some kindergarten teachers organize their classes as armies.

True madness is an achievement denied to many who are merely casually mad.

Organization is vulnerable differently; some ways of organizing something yields only to extreme force; others collapse when you breathe on them.

All organization leaks; where it leaks from is critical.

Some people can organize themselves; others require a guide or mentor; others require a dictator, a tyrant.

Sometimes organization coincides with how something is put together; sometimes it coincides with how something can be taken apart.

Some people's ideas are exquisitely organized but their actions are a chaotic mess.

It is easier organizing something complex than something simple;

It is easier to organize something badly disorganized than to reorganize something someone else has organized badly.

Organization regulates the flow of something. "What?" is the question? Some organization regulates the flow of questions; some organization regulates the flow of answers. Often these are different organizations.

Some people believe they are organizing an elephant when they are really organizing a crow.

The organization of words is easy; organizations of emotions harder; the organization of words is always done accomplished with other words. The organization of emotions is never organized with words but only actions.

Organization begins often starts organizing nothing for a start and moves from one nothing to the next.

The simplest things may have the most complex organization.

Along with every known is an expected; along with every unknown is an unexpected; along with every unknown unknown there is an unexpected unexpected.

Something are disorganized uniformly, others randomly.

There are degrees of organization— except for the person you love;

There are ways of being organized that mock organization;

You always have options about what you organize and how much. Sometimes you have options about what you organize but not how or how much. Sometimes you have options about how much you organize but not what.

Organization is in the I of the beholder.

Organization is held by the things organized.

Incoherent principles may produce a coherent organization.

The lowest levels of an organization is the recipient of organization; who receives organization varies; sometimes it the person on the bottom; sometimes it is the person on top;

Some people believe they are organizing an elephant when they are really organizing a crow.

Organization is a matter of what touches what. There is geometry to organization disguised as topology; often the topology of organization disguises itself as geometry.

We organize to be prepared but often for the wrong thing.

It is easier to organize an assault than surrender.

Some organization depends on inertia; other organization depends on acceleration, others on freaky quantum forces.

Clarity means giving up something, sacrificing something precious.

All organization is a compromise between preferences and necessity.

No organization begins at the beginning. Every organization can only begin when there is some organization to start with.

Clarity always comes as a picture puzzle that must be put together before you see what it is a picture puzzle of.

How is it possible for two people to see the same thing with absolute clarity and see two different things.

Seeing something clearly and acting on it clearly are two different things.

Clarity is a tax on action that not many of us are willing to pay.

Sometimes clarity is beside the point.

Sometime we reach for clarity with a closed fist.

Frequently there is clarity at the beginning and sometimes at the end; but it is most often missing in the middle where it is needed most.

Clarity seldom comes after a rich dinner and a roll in the hay.

We depend on our strengths to discover our weaknesses but our weaknesses to discover our strengths.

Changing means changing exactly the parts of ourselves that we depend on the capacity to change anything at all.

If we had a good measure of them, our routines would appear different.

A man without a style is just badly dressed; a woman without a style is naked.

It is possible to covet a brother's style more than a brothers wife.

Sometimes it takes a long time and considerable effort to stay unclear and completely fogged up about something.

We are likely to become clear about something only the instant it changes into something else.

There are different kinds of clarity. There is the clarity of a man in love. There is the clarity of a Zen master. Then there is the clarity of a bug at the end of a pointed stick.

You can tell a clear headed man in a crowd. He is the one watching his feet.

Clarity is a spinning bubble balanced on the tip of a pin.

The opposite of clarity is two other opposite clearer clarities.

Art is always a clarity but about what is unclear.

Clarity always comes in a package; sometimes wrapped as a surprise, sometimes as a scribbled reminder.

Self-knowledge depends on a recklessness with those parts of ourselves that we are most careful and cautious about.

It is changing ourselves that requires most dependence on other people.

The grand bulk of our routines are incomplete. They are approximations, at best.

Style is sometimes a matter of under dressing, sometimes a matter of going naked.

Style is mostly a matter of how you incorporate randomness in your life, a matter of how you handle gaps, breaks and asymmetry.

The most creative people make their routines into a style.

Style gives traction, creates a friction; what makes it a style is what it creates friction between.

Living a style and seeing it on someone else are two different things;

A new technology surprises only those people who do not use it.

Even self-delusion has a style to it.

Sometimes a style is like a lens that focuses a person

Each of us harbors at least one desire that only a new technology can satisfy and another desire that the new technology will frustrate completely.

What technologies does God use?

Any technology has a center and a point furthest away from it's center. It takes a while for a new technology to find the furthest away from its center.

Every new technology discovers and creates its own rationale.

A technology built on sand/wood can be as strong as one build of steel.

Every technology builds on, anchors and strengthen a human weakness.

The weakest point of a technology is always the beginning of a new technology.

A technology embeds itself in its users.

For the first generation of users a technology holds no surprises

The infancy of a new technology corresponds to the old age of the technology it supplants.

There is no technology ahead of its time

The excuses for not using a technology disappear suddenly.

How a technology appears to us is a feature of the technology.

A technology is seldom completely replaced by another technology.

The ghost of an old technology always is around to frighten the inventors of a new technology

One cost of a new technology is always the old technology it replaces.

The birth of a new technology establishes the birthday for a generations.

What a technology is and what a technology does are separate only at the instant a technology begins.

We should beware of technology that extends only a single piece of ourselves.

We believe in a technology because it is there.

The longest distance any technology travels is from outside of us to inside of us.

The greatest trick any technology manages is to become invisible.

The gap between technologies is always measured in generations.

The youngest people frightened by a technology is a good measure of how new innovative and powerful a technology is.

Some technology changes from the inside out others from the outside in. And some from the top down others from the down up.

Breaking is a machine's way of saying no.

A generation is defined by the devices it aspire to and the devices it has been deprived of by its current technology.

The success of a technology does not depend on how well it satisfies a human need.

A new technology is a reflection of power in any society.

Any gap in technology is rapidly filled with a new technology.

Every technology is a heap a hedge, a network.

The gap between technologies is always measured in generations.

Technologies breed; every technology requires another technology to help it grow.

A new technology surprises only those people who do not use it.

The user of a technology is often not the person who feels its effects the most.

The major effects of a really new technology shows up at the far edges of its reach.

Every technology breeds; most often new technologies. The most innovative technologies breed new users.

When it comes to technology there are no unintended consequences.

Some technology changes from the inside out others from the outside in. And some from the top down others from the down up.

It is easy to confuse the personality of the machine with its functionality; the functionality of a device masks its personality. The study of the personality of machines is a science waiting to be born.

In the struggle between the personality of a device and the personality of its user the user loses.

Which of us will stand up when the cry goes out, "machines arise?" Which of us should?

One day we shall build a machine with a brain and it will turn out to be not a lot like us.

Every machine device comes with a virtual device in which it is embedded. A virtual device carries with it a world in which one must be prepared to live. We operate with the virtual device; the real device is hidden from us.

For us, our machines are the great force of nature.

There is justice in the large and justice in the small. Justice in the small is likely to be mistaken for a pebble in your shoe.

For whom is the algorithm law?

A law that pleases no one must satisfy someone.

Nothing is so completely natural and so fully enwrapped in the world that some law does not apply.

When then law gives birth it always gives birth to twins.

The law is the appearance of justice.

The law consists entirely of gaps which are filled with more law.

The height of the law occurs when it makes whole again something that was smashed into a million indistinguishable pieces – most likely by the law.

The law seeps into the world and hardens slowly.

What can one reasonable demand of the law? Nothing without permission.

The form of the law is much less mutable than the law itself.

The law has many opposites not a few of which require the law to exist. The opposite of law is not chaos—even chaos requires laws to operate.

Few people live in a place so far away from everywhere that soneone's law does not reach.

The law never forgets —although it never remembers completely either.

Any law can always be balanced on the head of a pin; but the law which can be balanced on the head of a pin may not be easily balanced on a table.

*The law cannot be applied in exactly the same way twice.
Every application of the law changes the law and the reality to
which the law can be applied.*

The law should be a mirror in which a people
can see themselves not a window through which
people look out at other people.

No wall can be erected around a castle that is
strong enough to keep the law out.

The prices of justice is always the cost of the
lawyer; sometimes it is the cost of the judge.

It is possible to say "I'm not that kind of lawyer"
and mean it.

The law is a measure of distance.most often the
distance from the street to the jail.

The law is the cost of justice.

Sometimes God gives us a gentle hint about
what is forbidden – about that which we should
not do. Other times he sends us a text while we
are driving.

The time you have for baking bread cannot be
spend making love.

Time always tangles and knots.

Waiting makes time available for anything

Some of us are who we always were; some of us are what we will ultimately become; there are others who are always in between.

A mirror is all the clock most people need to tell time.

The only important measure of time is how long it takes for the crop to ripen.

There are always pieces of time left over from any job but never enough to complete the job.

So many choices, so little choice.

There is a time for reaping and a time for sowing but the time for reaping is always in the future and the time for sowing in the past.

The time for remembering is always in the future; the time for forgetting is always now.

He counted up to 4 trillion, then recounted to make sure he had it right, then let go.

There is never enough time to evolve completely. No species has enough time to evolve completely. Evolution takes more time than any species is allotted.

Only a mad man counts in dog years or tells time in inches.

There is always more time than we can use and less than we need

When his time went up in smoke he saved the ashes.

How old is a dog in frog years?

Some time happens in the head, some in the heart.

Some people have the ability to fold time in cute little packages. Others can only knot time in tangles.

Some of us time as if there was no tomorrow; and for some of us this is true.

Time can be filled with anything; some of us fill the time between gaps with other gaps.

Some people hear about an event before it happens, some after it happens, some while it is happening; and some people never hear about an event even when they are a part of it.

Some of us are who we always were; some of us are what we will ultimately become; there are others who are always inbetweeen.

The gap between desire and need is often filled by something that satisfies neither.

100

The most expensive watch and the cheapest tell the same time differently.

Linear time and circular time require different watches

The calendar tells time differently than a watch.

You can fake a second but not a moment.

Time often appears in a disguise.

There are always pieces of time left over from any job but never enogh to complete the job.

There is always enough time for pain or to make a mistake.

One persons before is often another's person's after and still another person's during.

There is a time for being restless and a time for settling down; telling the difference is difficult.

To tell a place you look around; to tell a time requires a different kind of looking;

Place remains the location of time as the remains of time resemble the remains of place.

Words words words. There is always something to say, there is always someone to say it. Hearing it is another matter.

An Idea sometimes resembles the person whose idea it is more than the things it is an idea about.

Having an idea and believing it are two different things.

There is no human surface that cannot be tiled with words.

Every loose end can be tied up with words

Every idea has a seam.

When words get tangled it is impossible to untangle them with other words.

Ideas are always incomplete. Completing them is always a problem. Sometimes the completion of an idea is a completely different idea from the idea it completes.

There is always a struggle between having an idea and an idea having you.

The blessing of logic is that it always shoots straight; the curse of logic is that it always shoots straight.

The beginning and ending of even a good idea may be a bad idea.

The world does not think; it could probably think if it had to but it doesn't have to.

Words cast shadows. It is in these shadows that ideas live.

Words are elastic enough so they can be
stretched and they are rigid enough so that they
can be welded together.

Actions dress themselves in words. Often this is
a disguise.

Words are sometimes the skeleton, sometimes
the skin.

What is a song but some words with a little
sugarcoating on top.

Words can be piled up in a shapeless heap.

Every idea is the visible tip of a theory in
disguise.

What is the engine of a word; The eyes? The
tongue?

Any good idea rests on a hidden structure. It
is this structure that makes it a good idea. And
this makes it nearly impossible to translate. We
must translate from one structure into another
structure; and neither structure is visible to us.

The memory of a word is often a different word
entirely.

Grammar controls words but only to a point.

Some writers are warmed by the friction between words. The friction between words keeps some readers people warm.

The same idea in a poem and an essay about food is a different idea.

A picture is worth maybe 37 extra-ordinary words made into a sentence, but at most only 5 common ones made into an abstract idea.

Do not hold words responsible for the ideas they make up.

Ideas are always swathed, sometimes in a fog, sometimes by cement. A significant part of every idea is hidden.

Shaking an idea loose from the baggage it comes with is the main problem with any idea.

Sometimes the idea of something is worth more than the something it is an idea of.

The idea of something bears only a family resemblance to the thing it is an idea of.

Ideas have a shape and a color and a size. Human ideas have a human shape, a human size, a human color.

The path along which even a good idea leads you can be twisted; you can get lost following even a good idea.

The space within which an idea travels from person to person is not the space in which the idea lives.

Sometimes ideas fly from place to place like a flock of birds; other times they crawl.

Sometimes you snatch an idea that is floating in the air, sometimes you have to scrape it from the ground.

Coming up with a new idea and getting credit for coming up with it are two different things.

He managed to do Escher in words but fell off when he stopped listening carefully.

Sometimes the train is going in the right direction only the rails are pointed the wrong way.

He lost the vitality he never had as a child, and with it, the intelligence he had never been able to use to make sense of things.

CORKSCREWS

a commentary

Every truth worth knowing can be said in no more than fifteen words. And any truth that can be said in no more than fifteen words can be said in six or less. Of course, any truth that can be said in six words or less is so obvious that it doesn't need to be spoken of at all. (It is also clear that truths that are so obvious they don't need to be spoken of, require no fewer than three volumes to write down.)

Corkscrew: 1.An instrument for opening bottles sealed with a cork.

2. An instrument for opening the mind to thought. 3. A self-illuminating light; illumination in chaotic motion.

Almost anything can pass itself off as information and anything that is not information can impersonate information and anything that is information about something can disguise itself as information about something else.

Directions, junk mail and revelations.

Ordinary information (DIRECTIONS.) Information is usually about something you can almost grab hold of, something you feel you can touch. At its most ambiguous, this kind of information seems to be about some-kind-of-thing-in-particular. Most every day, run of the mill information is of this sort — otherwise why bother.

Informationless information (JUNKMAIL.) Some information is quite different though: it seems to be information about nothing at all. After you come to know it, after you use it to become informed you seem to be in exactly the same position vis a vis the world that you were before you knew it. Much of the news on television seems to be of this kind.

Extraordinary information (REVELATIONS)

Still other information seems to tell you about everything. After you receive it you seem to know a little more about everything; everything seems a little different. Although you can't point to anything that specifically informed you about anything, everything feels different, you see everything a little differently. Then there are Corkscrews.

The compression of information.

Information compression is a significant topic. It has seldom been subjected to any interpretation. On the other hand there is a powerful scientific community working at improving data compression techniques. In this world of real limits on data storage and on channel capacity, data compression is of practical importance.

Compression of information involves conserving the amount and kind of information by changing the way it is represented in order to reduce the cost of storing or transmitting it. Data compression is a matter of rhetoric, elocution and diction, except the saying may be in a code not made for speaking.

Like dieting, simply shedding weight is not the decisive thing in data compression. The trick is to peel away the excess mass but do so in a way that does not compromise the integrity and essentials of person or message; losing 20 pounds by chopping off a head or an arm or other piece of ones anatomy would be an unacceptable weight loss program.

Figuring out powerful coding systems which allow for the efficient transmission of information is a major intellectual achievement. There is much science in this and not a little art. Effective compression of data involves discovering and eliminating redundancy. It involves avoiding saying some-

thing or even hinting at something even a fraction more than once. It entails
finding a way to say something in a shorter way, in fewer symbols or words, or using no words or symbols at all. It is an issue of efficiency, of conservation.

Of course, it is possible to set one's mind on saying the same thing in different ways for variety, or the same thing in a longer more elegant, distinctive way for emphasis. And really effective compression of information might involve figuring out how to say a million different things in the same way showing that they were in fact the same thing even though they looked different. Which brings us to the nub of the matter.

It is the involvement of machines in the information process that has raised this issue to the level of significance and importance it has now.

As long as we were dealing mostly with other humans data compression was not problematic — we could get away with murder, and did. Within the range of human meanings and experience we compressed data furiously and shamelessly. As long as the demand for efficiency was held in human constraints and worked in human contexts that were shaped to respect human limitations and satisfy the interests of human communities in social contexts, no machine could come close to compressing data the way we humans naturally compressed data — in wild, world sized chunks.

But as we began to use machines more, especially computers, as we began to need great globs of information continuously and instantaneously, as our science began to require unbroken streams of information from far away planets, from the insides of atoms; as our economies became dependent on real time information about all economic transactions; as our medicine demanded that the human genome be mapped completely and totally, the human compression of communication became inadequate. No human context could cope with the range of data we were forced to compress; nor was the range of human experience wide enough to encompass the technic of compression;

analytic, computer assisted compression came to be required and significant.

At the interface between human and machine the shape and form of communication remained constrained by human limitations, by how fast we can read or hear or type or speak; at the interface, human limitations dominate. The machines are bound by our limitations.

We realized quite early that because we needed to deal with computers only at the interface, we did not need to impose our limitations on them (although lending them our strengths was a different matter) and we could let our machines transmit information between themselves and calculate with information in whatever form was most advantageous to them even though it was completely incomprehensible to us. By giving up access to this intermediate forms of information we developed for machines to use — and ultimately, the data forms the machines developed for their internal use — we lost another element of control and, of course, our machines became one more degree unintelligible to us.

Human compression of information:

Humans have always compressed information. We have always worked hard at packing as much information as we could into our communications. We strive for efficiency and effectiveness naturally — not all the time every time, but consistently.

Humans compress information in different ways. One way by which we achieved compression by leaving unsaid what could be understood as being said only later, long after it was said, and, by not hearing those things when they were said. Humans achieve efficiency by compression on both sides of the communication divide — both on the speaking and the listening side.

Another way we compressed information was to shape the context that a person used to comprehend the messages we sent. First we learned that the more we could shape the context others used to comprehend our communications the more compressed
our speech could be. Then, after we learned to use context to control information, we learned the trick of assuming a context and assuming the other person to whom we were going to communicate could figure out the context we were assuming they would use — so that we never had to use any words to communicate context at all. We learned to make context self-defining. Of course, context depends on community, on a history, a line of connection to our fellows.

Humans also managed to compress information by using silence to communicate information. Humans learned very quickly that "nothing" could communicate enormous amounts of information if it was used in the right way. It is the management of silence that really distinguishes human compression of data.

In their management of silence humans have broken the back of scientific limitations on the compression of information. It is our capacity to make silence carry information and a lot of it, to let the unstated be a clue to the implied, to make what is not said constitute evidence of what might be said, and hence what is said by omission, that distinguishes human speech.

The length of silences, the shape of silences and attachment of silence to speech, silence as a commentary, silence as complement and criticism, all allowed a large number of ways of compressing information to nothing at all; even though were slower than machines we were cunning out of all proportion to our brain size, and our nature let us compress words into silences that spoke volumes.

Human compression of information by using shared and understood context and silence were two kinds of data compres- sion humans used. There is another a different kind of compres- sion of information, a compression in which information is com- pressed by manipulating something else other than information. We call them corkscrews.

Most of the corkscrews we encounter are aphorisms. it is in the form of epigrams that we are most familiar with cork-screws.But many works of art have the same quality; and occasionally other works — a good scientific theory, for example — do the same thing; Corkscrews seem a good general term for this kind of compressed package of information.

The term corkscrew is meant to convey a recursiveness, a continuous folding back on itself of something which no matter how closely packed, avoids touching itself but which is always asymptotically close.

As mechanisms for compressing information, corkscrews differ from silence and context in two ways:

• What is moved around is not only information about the world but also simultaneously, through the information about the world, some kind of information about information itself.

•The process of decompression of information is different. Silences and context are decoded — information is extracted — in a single, explosive reflexive stroke. But a corkscrew unwinds and unfolds strewing information in its path; information self- extracts, uncoils in a continuous process that takes time but is self-regulating, which occurs without attention, occurs like an unfolding. It self disassembles, then self assembles itself, then disassembles and reassembles itself again, in the mind. Like the purest information its contents emerge, become information only in the unfolding.

Here are some examples of corkscrews. Darkness also travels at the speed of light.

In a pinch you can use a hammer as a screwdriver but only once per screw.

It is bizarre that people will believe anything as long as you can prove it to them.

Sex is a pleasure; good sex is pleasure; great sex is what pleasure is about.

Armies never surrender at night.

The warning shot warns the shooter.

Folly is intelligence with a thorn in its paw. Great novelists die in other people's sleep.
The virtuous whore is the invention of the virtuous pimp.

Babies are nature's way of explaining sex in exactly the same way in which fat is nature's way of explaining food.

What is a corkscrew, really?

A corkscrew shows you an idea then it shows you the pattern in the idea then it shows you the pattern without the idea.

1. A corkscrew shows you an idea. Like any affirmative declarative sentence a corkscrew shows you an idea, presents an idea to you. It presents you with information about the world.

2. But a corkscrew shows you the pattern of an idea. Unlike most sentences which display an idea, a corkscrew shows you the pattern of the idea it displays, It makes the flesh of the idea translucent so you can discern its anatomy, see its bones, identify the underlying structure that gives it shape. A corkscrew presents you with information about the information it is presenting to you.

3.A corkscrew shows you the pattern without the idea. After a corkscrew presents an idea and the pattern of the idea it goes one step further; it displays the pattern without the aid of the idea it is the pattern of. A corkscrew presents you with information about the information it presented you. A corkscrew is information and meta information in the same package.

A corkscrew goes one step further than the edge of meaning; it makes the bones transparent and shows you the pattern without the idea, it dissolves the presentation of the pattern and leaves the pattern visible as a tracing on the mind itself, like a fossil in stone. Corkscrews work by blurring the line between information and information about information and information about information about information. Normally any pattern in sentences beyond the grammar, beyond poetry, is overwhelmed by the information the sentence carries. But in a corkscrew the words are arranged so that the information about the world is held at bay and is prevented from creating so strong a meaning as to overwhelm something else. What is this something else? It is a pattern of an idea around which words cling. Because the meaning of the world is held at arm's length a corkscrew allows the idea to emerge to throw off words so to speak and emerge in their own light.

In a corkscrew, indirection, misdirection, equivocation, ambiguity and distraction are all instruments of information transmission. A corkscrew works in just the opposite way of ordinary information and makes the opposite kinds of demands the person using it. It depends on managed ambiguity, engineered, controlled unclarity, disciplined disorganization.

What is true about the world is that everything is happening at once; Human beings know this and participate in it. This parallel processing goes along with the constant compression and decompression of information, with the use of information on a variety of levels simultaneously.

We parallel process naturally. We sing and chew gum and produce white blood cells and make love and fantasize at the same time. Yet we cannot think in this way. Consciousness demands a linear, exclusive process. Yet we are always engaged in a dozen activities simultaneously. When the parallel simultaneous implications and meanings are represented in some fashion, in a set of words a sentence, we speak of a corkscrew. Corkscrews, or information like them, hold the information we need to do this parallel processing. Corkscrews then, are a kind of music of thought (because theme and variation and harmony and development are all graspedatonce.)

Folding

Corkscrews depend on an ability humans have which is magical but quite natural. It involves the ability to fold information onto itself in informational space in an almost supernatural way. Information about the world is folded together with information about the information then the folded material is wound around an idea and tucked away in a set of words. The magical part of a corkscrew is that once taken in as information it unfolds in the mind, drawing information through the mind pushing and pulling it around in the brain. A corkscrews is a miniature, moving light, an illumination that is never still, that dances and sings over a landscape illuminating different parts of the ground terrain.

Here are instructions for this mental origami. Take a set of words and organize them so that they press against themselves, Set up some interference pattern so that the meaning of the words is blocked or distorted, so that the meaning of the words is interfered with. What is left of the words, is the pattern they make up, a pattern that only some of the meaning of the words represents.

Errors

Our brains do not process information the way our models tell us brains process information. Our models are just that, models, representations of something, in this case representations of processing information. Our representations work in symbolic space and time; to use them ultimately we map our calculations onto another representation — ultimately visual or tactile or auditory (what we see or what we feel or hear). Truth for us is merely the degree of fit between these two representations.

What this means is that we ought never fall into the trap of treating our representations as the real thing however

116

good they are at letting us predict the real thing, which is what they are designed to do. Our representations are designed to simulate the real thing. The better they do this the more we have faith in them. The danger is, of course the more faith we have the more likely we are likely to confuse reality with models of reality, to confuse faith in a models with a belief in the reality of the model.

We make our models to represent that reality to allow us to predict the reality; then we use it to make the prediction. The more accurate the model the more likely we are drawn into the trap that the model is the reality (rather than an effective representation of it) the more likely we are to make the tragic intellectual mistake of confusing the map with the territory. Each generation faces this problem in a different guise. This is ours. Information about reality is not reality.

We must build our models of reality up piece by piece gradually, whereas reality works in one fell swoop. Our models like our computers are mostly serial processors; Seriality is all we can handle; reality is parallel; everything is happening at once.

A lesson about information compression through three examples of corkscrews

"In a pinch you can use a hammer as a screwdriver but only once per screw."

Taken by itself this sentence seems to state one of the first principles that govern the transformation of quality into quantity. The idea that a hammer can be used as a screwdriver forces you to think about fundamentals. A coarse smashing motion can
be substituted for a delicate rotation motion. The universe is a pragmatic, flexible place — up to a point.

That point is when you act on it. Then something changes.

You get nothing for nothing in this world. There is a cost. The universe has a monopoly on fundamental laws. It is when you have to remove the screw that the lesson of the world comes home to you. You can use a hammer as a screw-driver only once per screw, not one and any small fractional number, certainly not twice.

To affirm that you can use a hammer as a screwdriver is to assert something about equivalent things, things that are identical interchangeable — but of course only up to a point. But the assertion forces you to consider the contexts the circumstances in which these two dissimilar objects can be the same.

This corkscrew is an assertion that such a context exists and an invitation to consider it. The only way it makes sense is if you simultaneously reexamine and perhaps redefine equivalence. The idea that this equivalence is bounded in time, that it only works once forces some further consideration.

Why this limitation? Is it in the nature of screw able things that are hammer able? Is it a matter of the nature of the directionality of the world, what can be done and undone? Is the lesson really that the use of a tool changes the entity on which the tools is used so that it is no longer manageable with that tool again. Does this statement convey information about hammers, about screwdrivers, about the stuff of the world or about all of these at once.

A corkscrew shows you an idea then it shows you the pattern of the idea and then it shows you the pattern itself without the idea.
"It is bizarre that people will believe anything as long as you can prove it to them."

What is this saying? It is about logic, and it is about believing, or about the ability not to believe, and it is about proof. In fact it is about all three of them together, so that the corkscrew raises an issue of what certainty and conviction looks like among humans.

People believe the most outrageous things. And the more outrageous the assertion they believe, the more they feel that they must believe these things, that they have no choice in the matter so long as you have proved the assertion to them.

This is the nature of proof, namely that once provided it compels belief. But proof is a sometime thing and this corkscrew talks to the issue of the logic within which something is proved as well as the construction of human beings who are compelled in their beliefs.

This conviction that they must believe is strongest when someone shows them that the assertion follows from something else they believe. The logic of this conviction is invisible, a silent, a-logical commitment.
"Sex is a pleasure; good sex is pleasure; great sex is what pleasure is about."

More than most corkscrews this corkscrew effectively compresses information on a number of levels. The trick — which is not a trick at all — is of course the twisty progression about pleasure — which is not a progression at all. This corkscrew uses pleasure to make sense out of sex and sex to make sense of pleasure — all in a single reasonable sentence. The idea that a particular something can express something generic is a little startling, so that the notion that good sex is pleasure or can be used to define pleasure, is surprising. But the progression twists on itself when it asserts that pleasure is about something and that great sex can be used to identify that which pleasure is about.
But what is pleasure about? It is about that which in one

instance is characterized by pleasure. The progression is shown— as so many progressions are — to be illusory.